How to Build a Property Portfolio Without the Banks

Escape the 9-5, Earn While You Learn and Build Property Wealth the Smart Way

David France

Get the Most Out of This Book

**At the back of the book
you will find download links to...**

A Free Deal Calculator
+
Free 4 Day Training

**With Compliments
from David France...**

Table of Contents

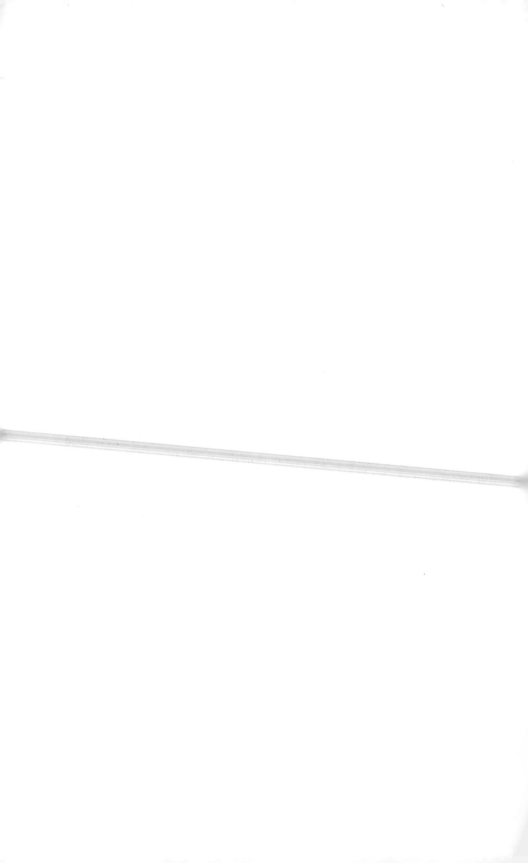

The NEW Way of Making Money in Property

Why You Should Read This Book

This book will show you how to get into property even if you have no money or experience, it is short but deceptively simple, inside its pages is the pathway to freedom and abundance. I know this to be true because both myself and my students have changed their lives dramatically in a very short period of time using the methods outlined in this book.

We are taught to go to school, work hard and if we are really lucky, get a good job. I want to show you another way, where you control your days, your earnings and your life!

These methods can lead to great wealth over time if you stick with them and in the shorter term can deliver a life of freedom. I have called the book 'How to Build a Property Portfolio Without the Banks' because I have gone from doing small deals worth a few thousand pounds in profit to doing large portfolio deals worth many 10s of thousands in profit per deal as well as owning a large property portfolio myself. This is what these methods can do for you.

The biggest thing that the property business can give you is freedom of time. The reason many of my students wanted to get into this business was to spend more time with their loved ones. What good is a high paying job if you have to work 80 hours a week?

I love picking up and dropping my son off at nursery every Monday, I like taking random Airbnb breaks with my family, I like taking a day off in the week to go to the park and have a bar meal, but one of my main vices is holidays, property has allowed me to travel the world several times visiting places like Hong Kong, Singapore, Thailand, Vietnam, Lao, Bali, Australia and the USA.

Maybe you want to help the poor, but you can only do this if you are not one of them, sure you can be kind and do nice things but if you really want to change people's lives for the better then you need wealth. Maybe you want material things like flash cars, nice clothes or you just want more choices in your life, then property can give you all that, I will show you how in this book using the NEW methods of buying and controlling property.

The New Way to Buy and Control Property

You may have read in the newspapers that the UK government is cracking down hard on landlords by taking away tax advantages, putting up stamp duty and so on. Landlords around the country are panicking and selling up. Buying property the old way has now become a high-risk strategy.

However, this is a golden time for property professionals who use the **New Way to Buy and Control Property**. Using the knowledge you will get inside this book you can take control of properties with very low risk and structure your business in a tax efficient manner.

This business can even be run remotely, I have bought and sold many overseas properties without seeing the properties or meeting the owners in person.

For me this business was never about the money even though I always wanted to be successful, it was about the choices and options you get when you are not in survival mode, you don't have to worry about money anymore, this is true empowerment, this is true freedom.

To your success

David France

How Property Changed my Life

I first got interested in property back in the days of the Sarah Beenie property shows. I always thought there was a lot of money to be made in property and at the time that was all I was thinking about because I could see I was on a path to nowhere.

I was working as a joiner getting paid £65 a day, and although I like the work and was quite good with my hands, it just wasn't enough money to live on. In the winter it was brutal, picking up pieces of wood covered with ice and the money wasn't even steady, so I had to further supplement my income by working as a lifeguard.

Every day I kept thinking 'I can't do this, there must be a better way', I could see the people around me and how their lives had turned out, never having enough money, not being able to take time off except for one holiday a year and constantly anxious about their finances and I could see that would be my future unless I did something about it.

So I chose property as my escape route and I knew there was no option but to succeed because I had nothing to lose, the worst that could happen was that it wouldn't work and I would have to keep working as a joiner. This mindset enabled me to keep going during all the struggles I had to go through to make this property thing work for me. I was relentless because on the one hand I could see a life of freedom and wealth and on the other a life of struggle, and that vision of how I wanted my life to be, kept me going where other people may have given up.

The reason my mindset was so important was this, things didn't happen for me overnight, it took two years before my property income was stable enough so I didn't have to take joinery work on the side to keep going, until the time I had lump sums coming in for months ahead and I could go full-time in my property business. The big advantage I had over some of my property coaching clients was that I didn't have a wife and family when I started, so the only pressure I was under was the pressure to free myself from having to take on work, so I could devote myself to property fulltime.

My Freedom Path

I started off with strategies I learned going on courses. The first course I went on was run by an Australian guy (who had 150 properties), and I worked out what he was making and really bought into the idea of having passive income streams from property, but three months after I got started the law changed and that strategy that I was using became mortgage fraud almost overnight, so after I had put in all that work I had to start all over again.

I had paid a lot of money for the course and at the time I had the grand total of £2000 to put into my property business so it was a huge blow, but as I will keep repeating, failure was simply not an option for me so I had to pick myself up and try something else.

I needed a way to be able to focus on property full-time without having to keep going back to joinery work to pay bills, that would give me the time to build up a passive income portfolio of properties, that would allow me to become free to do what I dreamed of, travel the world while making money from property.

On the next course I attended I learned how to use lease options to take control of properties I didn't own, and this time everything clicked. Using lease options to secure properties and then packaging deals to sell on would bring in the income I needed to go full-time in property. I started implementing these strategies and I loved it. I was helping people who were often in a desperate situation and they were so appreciative, and it felt good to be doing something that people needed so badly.

I felt like I was in the groove because I was making good money and it felt really good when people made comments after doing the deal like, "I can't believe you've taken this burden off my shoulders, I was panicking, I couldn't sell it through the estate agent and you've come along and you've worked a solution out which I didn't know about that's all legal, and somebody else has got the property so they're going to make some money from it and you've solved my problem."

It really is a win-win situation because these people are burnt out, they are sick and tired of property and I know how to help people who can't sell their homes both in the UK and overseas.

I completely understood how these people felt because at one stage I was that frightened property owner who had a problem property overseas. I'd bought a cheap property in Detroit and it didn't take long before I realised I'd made a big mistake.

The property was always falling vacant, there were lots of problems and communicating with the agents was a nightmare. So, on a long trip to the USA with my girlfriend (now my wife), we decided to take a detour to Detroit to visit the property which was vacant at the time.

We got the keys from the agent and couldn't believe it when we rolled up to the house, the neighbourhood was really dodgy and the house had been broken into and vandalised and the boiler stolen. We decided to stay and fix up the house, (this is where my joinery skills were really a godsend), and when it was done I listed it on Ebay for 30 days where it sold pretty much straight away for £17,500 and I made back the money it had cost me. But it was a scary time until the house was sold.

I had been doing these lease option deals and selling them on for a while and began building a reputation for being a 'good guy' in the industry. My deals were going through smoothly and the vendors and buyers were happy and started sending more deals my way, the solicitors involved in these deals started recommending me and my business started to take off.

But the faster you grow, the bigger mistakes you can make. You can pay a big price if you don't know what you are doing, because if you do it the wrong way or get involved with the wrong people it can cost you everything. I wish there was someone who would have mentored and trained me on the right way to do things back in the early years and saved me from some of my mistakes. Luckily, I got out from under some deals that went badly wrong and learned some very valuable lessons about doing due diligence on the people you go into business with.

I'm now at a point in my life I could have only dreamed of, it's not the big house or nice car that's important to me or the fact I am able to live a comfortable life. What's important is my wife and two kids and being able to provide for them and leave them a legacy. I now own a decent sized portfolio which throws off enough income so I don't have to work if I don't want to, but I enjoy what I do, putting larger portfolio deals together, packaging them up to sell and adding to my portfolio when I come across properties that meet my criteria. I also love mentoring and helping others, I want everyone to be able to change their lives through property.

The first phase for most of my clients is to help get them out of their jobs, and that can be challenging because some have families and need to work and have to do this business in their spare time around home and work obligations. That's why with my clients I focus on cashflow first, the dream of passive income is all very well, but it takes time and money to build up. Finding and packaging deals to sell on is the quickest way I know to bring in decent money to free people from their jobs, and then over time, as they gain in contacts and experience they can build long term wealth through a property portfolio.

So now you know my story but the big takeaway I hope you get from this book, is that literally anyone can do this business and build property wealth while making a good income along the way, as long as they realise that it takes some time and effort and keeping the vision of the life they want to build constantly in mind, while they keep moving forward. If I can do it anyone can!

The Rent to Rent Strategy Explained: A Cash Flow Strategy

How to make ongoing monthly cashflow from other people's property without needing deposits or a mortgage.

So, what is Rent to Rent?
Simply put, it's where you rent property from a landlord at a low fixed monthly rent and then you go ahead and rent it out using rental strategies that produce a higher monthly income. Your profit is the difference between the rent you pay the landlord and the monthly running costs and the rent you're able to achieve.

With Rent-to-Rent you are offering the landlord a guaranteed rent every month and usually offering to cover the repairs on the property as well for a fixed period of time, the longer the term you get the more money you can make, the average term is between three and five years with a break-clause in some cases.

You can use the Rent-to-Rent strategy on any property, single let houses, houses of multiple occupation (HMO), serviced accommodation (SA) and commercial properties.

Here is an example of one way of making money with Rent-to-Rent but remember this strategy is limited only by your imagination.

John Smith (the owner) has a 2 bedroom fully furnished apartment for rent in Manchester City Centre that he owns with no mortgage on it, it is in a small building and in a very good location near bars, restaurants and shopping. John is asking £750 per month and advertising the property on Open rent www.openrent.co.uk and trying to find a tenant himself.

Along comes Darren Styles (the investor) and finds John's property while searching the portal. He contacts John directly as this property meets Darren's criteria, Darren wants to make cashflow so he can leave his job quickly and rather than save up big deposits to buy property he decided Rent-to-Rent will help him get there much quicker.

Darren has been well-trained and uses a calculator to work out how much he can make by renting the property out by the night, he knows the nightly average in Manchester is £110 a night and he will get about 70% occupancy over the year.

He factors in the running costs that he will need to pay such as cleaning, TV licence, water, electric, Wi-Fi etc, plus the booking fees for the portals like Booking.com and Airbnb. He realises he will net £750 per month! Darren asks John if he is open to a long-term let on the property and tells John EXACTLY what he plans to do with the property and offers him full market rent for the next three years! This is a no-brainer for John as he gets a tenant for three years with no void periods and no repairs to worry about.

You might think well why doesn't John just do this himself?, Well most landlords want PASSIVE income and no hassle, running a property like this is called a serviced apartment (SA) and requires more time, and another skill-set and lets be frank some landlords are just plain lazy!

See the exact calculation we use next to work out the profit.

ONLY CHANGE VALUES IN RED	
Serviced Accommodation Calculator Based Upon Occupancy	
Tenant Payment (Rent)	750
Brokers Finders Fee £	0
Other Costs	0
Total Rent Earned £	2342.08
Total Startup Costs £	0
Monthly Profit £	756.66
Return On Investment	#DIV/0!
Monthly Running Cost £	1585.43
Accommodation Rate Per Night £	110
Average 70% Occupancy Rate (Days)	21
Rent In Bookings Per Calendar Month £	2342.08
Gas & ElectricricSupplies & Check Ins	53.23
Council Tax	110
Digital TV & Broadband/ WIFI	62
Water	30
Cleaners Cost - Based on 2 day stay av	228.89
Booking Platform Fee	351.31
Startup Cost £	0
Brokers Finders Fee £	0
Letting Agent Admin Fee & Bond	0
Portal Setup Fee	0

What Paperwork is Used?

Depending on the type of deal you do, a Management Agreement is the most common type of agreement, which has the provision to sublet, which is crucial to this strategy.

Things to Check

If you are turning a Rent-to-Rent to a serviced apartment you must make sure you will not have any issues with the block management company, (usually the freeholder), as some do not permit short-term lets, so be sure to raise this point with the owner and get any necessary consents prior to committing to this type of deal

If the property has a mortgage on it the owner must also check his terms and conditions to make sure he is not breaching them by letting to you.

You may have heard of something called Article 4 which means you need planning permission on some properties depending on the use, a serviced apartment however is not governed by Article 4 as the serviced accommodation is not classed as someone's primary residence, therefore planning permission is not needed.

A friend of mine has a big business (doing millions of pounds in revenue), where he does Rent-to-Rent on a massive scale, he finds large employers that need short-term accommodation for their employees (like EDF, BAE, etc.) and then finds large properties and rents them by the room to these contractors. He make a huge margin between what he pays the landlord and what he gets from the contractors, he is now expanding into Europe with this model, it just shows you where you can go with this if you want to go BIG!

Doing the above may mean you have to have a HMO licence so be sure to check with the local council before you enter any type of arrangement with a landlord, also make sure the property is safe and has fire safety features like fire doors and fire extinguishers, (read more here: https://www.gov.uk/government/collections/fire-safety-law-and-guidance-documents-for-business).

If you are looking to leave your job fast, then maybe you only need 4-5 of these properties, or if you are like my friend then the sky is the limit and you can take this to a whole new level.

Why not start with your financial freedom figure and work on replacing this first, then you can set more adventurous goals as you hit each milestone, that way the end goal is much more achievable.

David's Rent to Rent Airbnb Case Study

Whitworth Street – Manchester – M1 6LQ

Agreed rent with owner £750 per month
Term 3 years with 12-month break clause

We put this on Airbnb and Booking.com and averaged out £110 a night and we get about 70% occupancy meaning we net after costs around £700 profit per month.

We found Maria (the owner) on Openrent.co.uk and she was happy with our offer as she is based in the Netherlands and was trying to self-manage this property from overseas, so our offer to take care of the maintenance and repairs throughout the whole three year term meant her profit goes way up and her hassle goes way down, which she is very happy with while we make a tasty monthly profit.

These deals are there to be done!

How to Use Lease Options Explained

Lease Options Explained, a Long-term Wealth Building Strategy, the New Way to Build a Large Property Portfolio.

This is where things get exciting, Rent-to-Rent is great for cashflow, but you will never get the benefit of capital appreciation, in this next strategy using the power of lease options however, you get both!

Let me expand on this, like a Rent-to-Rent property you 'lease' the property for a period of time and have the 'option' to buy in the future at a pre-determined price but NOT the obligation to buy, this is huge and means you can walk away if you decide not to buy the property.

Common names for a lease option in the property world are Lease Option Agreement (LOA), Lease Option (LO) and Purchase Lease Option (PLO).

Just like Rent-to-Rent you have a management agreement, but you also have an 'option' agreement which states the fixed price you can buy the property for in the future.

How do you make money with Lease Options?

You make cash flow on lease options in the same way as in Rent-to-Rent and you must make sure you get as long a term on the agreement as possible, so in Rent-to-Rent three to five years is a common term for the length of the lease, with a lease option you can take the length of term as long as you can get the seller to agree, however if a mortgage is on the property the option to buy price must be within the mortgage term, i.e. no longer than the term of the mortgage.

With a nice long option term, let's say ten years you know you can make cashflow for the next ten years and when house prices go up you can exercise the option (the right) to buy and make a capital gain.

See the graph below which shows house price growth since 1952, we all know house prices whilst they can go down as well as up, in the long term double on average every 7-10 years (in certain areas we call 'hotspots').

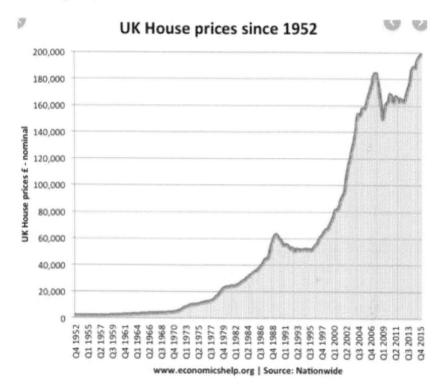

UK House prices since 1952

www.economicshelp.org | Source: Nationwide

Let me give you an example of a lease option in action

Phil Maxwell has a property he bought in 2007 (at the peak of the last crash) and the property is in Birmingham 200 miles away from where he lives. Phil thought it would be a great investment but his focus is on his job as an IT contractor and he employed a letting agent who was not very competent. The tenant stopped paying the rent and the property also started to fall into disrepair. Phil had to go through the process of evicting the tenant which caused him a lot of emotional stress and the property was now vacant and needed fixing up, so his losses were running into thousands of pounds.

Not surprisingly, Phil became completely disenchanted with property and just wanted out!

Here are the figures.

Phil paid £72,000 for the property but it is only worth £65,000, the mortgage payment is £201 a month and the property when fixed up will rent for £550 a month and the mortgage expires in 23 years.

We offered to take the pain away from Phil and fix up his property, our offer looked like this…

£1 paid to the seller (option consideration)

Purchase price £72,000

Term 22 years

Monthly payment (lease fee) £201

Why doesn't he just sell the property? Well after selling costs he would lose money on this property.

See the deal calculation we use to work out how profitable a Lease Option can be

Lease Option Deal Machine	
Rent Per Calendar Month £	500
Monthly Payments £	201.00
Purchase Price £	72000
Interest Rate	3.00%
Sourcing Fee £	0
Legal's £	750
Refurb Costs £	3500
Total Purchase Costs £	**4250**
Total annual rent £	6000
Total mortgage £	201.00
10 % lettings fee	50.00
Casfflow after letting agent fee	450.00
Net Cash Flow £	**249.00**
Net Annual Return	**2988**
Investor Return	**70.31%**

The returns are staggering, 70.31% ROCE (Return on Capital Employed), so the total output cost on this deal is £4,250 with a monthly return of £249. In 17 months the deal would achieve break-even point.

Now an investor will have to do repairs and ongoing maintenance and have to manage the property properly to get the best returns but if you compare a lease option to a 'normal' buy-to-let property there is no 25% deposit (£18,000) to be paid, no stamp duty and no credit checks from lenders or commitment to long-term debt. You get cashflow and capital growth in the future with a normal buy-to-let but with lease options you get the same outcome but much less risk.

Advantages of Lease Options over Normal Buy-to-Let
£1 down to secure the deal (£1 minimum)
No mortgage needed
No deposit needed
No stamp duty payable

Bad credit ok
Anyone can buy
Huge leverage

You could buy at least four lease options based on the above numbers using the deposit you would have put down on just one property!

What Paperwork is Used?

The basic paperwork that is used is as follows

Heads of Terms (HOT)

This is the very first piece of paperwork that is put together and has the buyer and seller details on it (name, address) and the terms of the deal including the purchase price, the term and the monthly payment and this gets signed by the buyer (investor) and seller and then sent to the solicitors to be drawn up into a contract.

Letter of Authority (LOA)

If a mortgage is on the property you need to get one of these signed by the seller so you can contact the lender(s) and confirm the mortgage details, balance and so on in order to protect your investment and make sure the mortgage does not have any arrears.

Management Agreement (MA)

This outlines the responsibilities of the buyer and seller while the agreement is running and has the provisions for repairs and other relevant matters.

Option Agreement (OA)

This document covers the purchase price agreed and how to exercise the option to buy and termination provisions.

Power of Attorney (POA)

With a power of attorney this covers what happens in the event the seller is uncontactable and can in some cases have a provision for the buyer to sign the TR1 transfer document, which is vital if they want to buy/sell the property when they come to exercise the option.

RX1 and UN1

Make sure you have a RX1 which is a restriction that gets lodged at the land registry which protects your investment and would stop a seller just selling the property in the future if they felt like it.

A UN1 is unilateral notice which makes everyone aware you have a lease option over the property and provides further protection.

Lease Options Offer Infinite Flexibility

You can do a lease option on residential properties, commercial properties, shops, blocks of flats, on land and properties both with or without a mortgage.

Ways to profit from a lease option:

1) You make cashflow over the term of the agreement.

2) You make a capital gain when house prices rise.

3) You can put in a Tenant Buyer (advanced strategy).

4) You can add value to the property.

5) You can sell your interest in the property for a fee.

6) You can make an ongoing Income packaging and selling your excess lease option deals to investors for fees.

A few important things to remember..

You do not need a mortgage-lender's consent to enter into a lease option as the paperwork is designed to comply with the mortgage terms and conditions.

Always use a solicitor to do these deals as these are investments and must be done properly, I can't tell you how many horror stories I hear where people try and do a deal with a seller around a coffee table as they have some 'template' agreement they got from a Facebook group just so they can save a few hundred quid in legal costs. This is short-sighted and will come back to bite you in the future. It is vital the seller gets legal representation and fully understands the implications of entering into a lease option with you.

Make sure your lease option is assignable as this will give you lots of choices, for example you get a year into the agreement and you decide you no longer want it, then you can simply assign it to someone else (for a fee).

Consent to Let

If seller has a buy-to-let mortgage it can be sublet, but if the property has a residential mortgage on it then you must make sure the owner gets CTL from the lender which will then allow you to sublet the property, most lenders will grant this.

Make payments direct to the lender where possible.

Why would a seller enter into this arrangement?

The hundreds of sellers we have helped by doing these types of deals can't thank us enough as they have become motivated and need our help, some of the motivations of sellers are…

Emigration
Repossession
Financial
Accidental landlord

Burnt out landlord
Divorce
Negative equity
Retirement

When should you not do a lease option?

In some instances, I strongly suggest you do NOT enter into a lease option such as,

A property does not stack up financially

The property does not produce cashflow, the mortgage product is unfavourable, the property is in too much negative equity or maybe the option term is too short.

A seller that is financially unstable

If a seller is about to go bankrupt or is in a real financial mess, with IVA's and lots of debts then it may not be wise to enter into a deal with them as this could affect the property in the future, as some other lenders have an 'all monies charge' in the terms and conditions, which means they can go after other properties the seller owns which could then impact your property.

A property that needs too much work

If you take on a property that needs too much work it may not be financially viable as if you have to put in lots of money to clear arrears or fix the property up, then you might as well have put the money down as a normal deposit on a property which defeats the purpose of doing lease options.

Controlling vs Owning

I hear many inexperienced and even some experienced investors talk down lease options by saying things like "well you don't actually own it", "the seller could change their mind at any time", "finding a lease option is like finding a needle in a haystack" and so on. It's clear they do not fully understand this strategy, you have far more leverage using this strategy than by using deposits to buy property, as this will take you much longer and at some point you will run out of cash however much money you have, restricting your ability to grow. By using lease options, you can build a large property portfolio very quickly using relatively small amounts of cash.

Ethics

Like every industry where lots of money can be made you will get people that take advantage of other people and lease options are no different, my advice is to treat a seller fairly and if they want your help and it makes sense to do a deal then go for it.

Dave's Lease Option Top Tips

If a seller has some mortgage arrears then talk to the lender on behalf of the owner and see if they will capitalise the arrears which will mean you do not have to pay the arrears off in one go up front, instead you add it to the total loan on the property.

If you come across a seller who has only a few years left on the mortgage, you can submit to the lender on behalf of the seller, a mortgage extension letter which asks the lender for an extra five years extension which can then make the deal work.

Dean's Story

Dean is in his mid-thirties and married to Laura, with two young children and living in Lincolnshire. He loves his job as a fighter pilot flying the Euro fighter-jet, but his job is very stressful, requires his complete focus and commitment and he works odd hours.

After many years working in the RAF Dean realised that if he wanted freedom in his life he needed to start planning for his future. For him, like most people it wasn't about having 'property millions', it was about having time-freedom and the financial wherewithal to work when he wants, take holidays when he feels like it and leave a legacy for his family without having to worry about paying the bills.

After careful consideration Dean realised property could be the vehicle for him to achieve this freedom as it can be leveraged and is a relatively safe, tangible asset unlike stocks and shares, cryptocurrency, forex etc. where with a click of a button your money vanishes.

Dean started doing his research and was drawn to me after watching my YouTube videos. He appreciated my straightforward approach and value-based video training.

(https://tinyurl.com/youtubedavidfrance).

Dean arranged a call with me where we discussed his various options and he mentioned he could get a job in Saudi Arabia earning £100,000+ per year but this would again mean being tied to a location, (in this case a foreign country) and still working long hours. He decided to start working with me with his goal to replace his current income and create a property portfolio while he continued working in his job.

Dean initially wanted to replace his salary by flipping property deals without having to buy them. This is a very safe method and different to how most people flip property, most people think you have to actually buy a property and get into debt to refurbish a property and then sell it to realise a profit, this is the hard way to make money and is risky. Dean followed our model which is to find a motivated seller and negotiate a really good deal, then secure the deal using paperwork and then trade that paperwork to an investor for a fee, meaning no mortgages, no deposits, no stamp duty, no debt and very little risk.

Dean also wanted something to leave his kids and he realised whilst flipping property is good for chunks of cash it will not make him rich, so he decided to build his portfolio by cherry picking the really good deals he was finding and making passive income from them whilst also building long term wealth.

Dean is still working as a fighter pilot and enjoys this job but has the skill-set to leave anytime he wants, as his part-time property career and his passive income from some of the properties he has in his portfolio now covers his all his living expenses.

Dean's Portfolio Building Using Lease Options Case Study

Lease Option Portfolio Building

Nottingham 4 bedroom detached
Portfolio acquisition for his legacy
Lease option structure
Agreed price £240,000
Market value £250,000
Monthly payment £374
Term 7 years
Market rent £900
Upfront payment to seller £12,000 (moving on money)

Lease Option Deal Machine	
Rent Per Calendar Month £	900
Monthly Payments £	373.00
Purchase Price £	240000
Interest Rate	3.00%
Sourcing Fee £	0
Legal's £	750
Upfront payment to seller	12000
Total Purchase Costs £	12750
Total annual rent £	10800
Total mortgage £	373.00
10 % lettings fee	90.00
Casfflow after letting agent fee	810.00
Net Cash Flow £	437.00
Net Annual Return	5244
Investor Return	41.13%

As you can see from above the ROCE (return on capital expended) is 41.13% and the cashflow is £437 after costs. If Dean bought this the 'normal way' he would have had to put down a 25% deposit which would be £75,000 plus stamp duty, whereas Dean has only had to outlay £12,750 in this case and get the same outcome.

Get 20%-50% Off Below Market Value Strategy

How would you like to get property at 20-50% discount?

Okay, so you might be thinking why on earth would anyone sell at 20%+ discount? Well we find many sellers that sell at 20%+ discount, in fact our main business is to package and sell these types of property deals to investors for a commission as we can't buy them all.

Why do people sell at a discount?

- ✓ Divorce
- ✓ Emigration
- ✓ Accidental landlord
- ✓ Burnt out landlord
- ✓ Chain breaks
- ✓ Financial problems
- ✓ Market uncertainty
- ✓ Problem property
- ✓ Leasehold issues
- ✓ Bad investment
- ✓ Tax changes (section 24)
- ✓ Portfolio landlords

Why do we insist on buying at a 20% discount (BMV)?

Trade Prices vs Retail Prices

You may have heard the saying you make your money when you buy, by buying property under market value you have these main benefits

- ✓ You can re-finance and pull out most of your funds very quickly so you can then buy another property, this is how professional investors build a large property portfolio fast.

- ✓ You buy at a trade price and can sell on for retail at any point you like.
- ✓ If the market falls (short term) you have a cushion.

How can you make money from this strategy?

- ✓ Buy the deal at a discount and sell on at the market-value making a capital gain.
- ✓ Find and secure a discount on a property (you do not need to buy it) and sell this as a 'package' to an investor who will pay you £3,000-£5,000 fee per deal.
- ✓ Buy the property at a discount and refinance the property and pull out your deposit

Dave's Top Tips
ALWAYS buy at a discount so you can recycle your deposits otherwise you will run out of cash.

Get good at raising finance so you can get more money for deposits so you can grow your portfolio big and fast.

Avoid flats and apartments as they usually have a higher turn-over of tenants and the service charges erode your profit, (buy freehold houses 3 bedroom+ with a garden).

Find buyers for your packaged deals you don't want using websites like LinkedIn

Don't get greedy with your fees, get the best fee you can for a deal but remember if you hold out for a top fee and don't get it, you get nothing.

Make sure solicitors can work to timescales set by sellers to avoid deals collapsing.

Take reservation fees from investors to secure a deal to avoid timewasters and losing deals.

For every three deals you find keep one and flip two using the fees to build your cash pot.

Aim for 7-10% gross rental yield

David's Below Market Value Case Study (Buy and Flip)

Nottingham

Market value £110,000

Agreed price £83,900

Discount 24%

Market rent £600

8.25% Gross Yield

We flipped this for £3,000 to an investor in London

See the calculator we use next

DEAL PROJECTIONS:
enter your estimates into the yellow coloured cells below...

INPUT - PURCHASE INFORMATION

Purchase Price		£	83,900.00
Stamp Duty	3.00%	£	2,517.00
Legal Fees		£	800.00
Refurb Costs		£	800.00

INPUT - BORROWING (enter 100 for deposit if not borrowing)

Deposit	20%	£	16,780.00
Mortgage	80%	£	67,120.00
Mortgage Arrangement Fee	3.00%	£	2,013.60
Mortgage Interest Rate	4.00%	£	230.45

INPUT - BTL INFORMATION (if applicable)

Monthly Rent		£	600.00
Letting Agent Fee	10.00%	£	60.00
Monthly Running Costs		£	15.00

INPUT - REFINANCE INFORMATION (if applicable)

New Market Value		£	110,000.00
Refinanced at (% LTV)	80%	£	88,000.00
Mortgage Arrangement Fee	3.00%	£	2,640.00
Mortgage Interest Rate	4.00%	£	302.13

INPUT - BTS INFORMATION (if applicable)

Sale Price		£	110,000.00
Home Report Fee		£	360.00
Legal Fees		£	1,000.00
Estate Agent Fee		£	1,000.00

DEAL ASSESSMENT

EXIT OPTION - BTL

Total Investment Cost	£	20,897.00
Monthly Cashflow	£	294.55
Gross Yield		8.58%
Net Yield		7.51%
Return on Investment		30.15%

EXIT OPTION - BTL (REFINANCING)

Refinanced monthly cashflow	£	222.87
Cash Out From Refinancing	£	20,880.00
Money Left in Deal	£	17.00
Months Before No Money Left in		0

EXIT OPTION - BTS

Total Investment Costs	£	20,897.00
Total Selling Costs (including 6 months mortgage)	£	3,742.67
Profit From Deal	£	16,226.73

Matthew's Story

Matthew is married with two children and lives in London and prior to getting into property his life was extremely stressful. His job while rewarding, required him to work a sixty-hour week and his family life was suffering.

His wife was very understanding about his long hours, but they spent very little family time together and he was missing out on time with his kids Freedie and Rana. His dream was to be able to pick them up from school and have mealtimes with them before bedtime. It was a simple dream but if you have kids you know how fast they grow up and before you know it they've left home and that time for bonding has passed.

Matthew started trying different make-money-from-home methods, he had a go at forex trading but lost all his investment which left him very sceptical and started him thinking about property. He knew you could make money in property as he had seen his own property rise in value over the years and like many people he had lots of equity but no cashflow. He decided he wanted to get into property but there were so many different directions he could take and he had no idea which one would be right for him.

He started watching YouTube videos and was drawn to my channel.

https://tinyurl.com/youtubedavidfrance

He was amazed at what you could do in property with very little money and was drawn to my down-to-earth approach and the fact that I make my living actually doing property deals not in the property education business as do some other educators.

He contacted me and explained his goal was to get his life back and we realised that sourcing and flipping property deals was the quickest path to him being able to leave his £60,000 a year job. We worked out that he only needed to put in about fifteen hours work a week and flip one to two deals a month to replace his income.

Matthew's Life Now

Matthew started with me in 2019 and after doing many property deals has a newfound level of confidence and zest for life. He has achieved his goal of having a family life and now takes his kids to school, picks them up, has his meals with the family and is able to talk about their days at school. His wife is much happier and they go on date nights every week.

Most people think about getting into property for how much money they can make, but Michael has achieved his most important goal which is a lifestyle goal, to get his family time back.

Matthew's Goals for the Future

Flipping property is great as it requires very little money and experience and can replace most people's income with just 1-2 deals a month, however if Michael stopped working he would have zero income, so building a property portfolio that produces a stable income is the next stage of his journey. He wants to build his legacy and future wealth by building his property portfolio for the passive income, he needs just ten properties to hit his goal and will do this in the next eighteen months following our methods.

The future looks bright for Matthew!

Matthew's Below Market Value Property Flipping Case Study

Matthew followed our training and his phone started to ring from what we call 'motivated sellers'.

A lady called who had inherited a property in Derby, this was a 2 bedroom mid-terrace property and it needed some work, the property had no mortgage and she needed the property sold quickly as she wanted to get her hands on the cash.

The figures were as follows...

Market value £90,000
Agreed price £72,000
(That's a whopping £18,000 equity from day one.)
Matthew's fee £3,000

Matthew made a £3,000 fee for simply taking a phone call from a motivated seller and negotiating a discount, he did not have to buy the property he just controls it using paperwork (a lockout agreement) and sells his interest to a property investor, meaning no mortgages, no deposits, no stamp duty, no risk!

The Assisted Sales Strategy Explained

What is an Assisted Sale?

As the name suggests you 'assist' the seller in selling the property, the aim is to get maximum value for the property and agree a fair price with the seller and make the bit in the middle (your profit), you have no stamp duty to pay because you are not actually buying the property so your risk is very low.

You must only work with motivated sellers and one of the main benefits you can offer a seller is you can 'advance cash' to them now instead of them waiting for a sale which can take months, so they can move on with their life right away.

We had one seller who was selling a unique property (a Church), they were going to convert this into flats and got planning permission but decided not to build and go to France instead to start a new life. Brexit was a concern and he wanted out fast, so we agreed on a £10,000 cash advance and he went to France to start a new life. In this particular case we also agreed to take care of the sale and split any profit 50/50, we then went to auction and sold it making a decent spread.

How can you make money with an Assisted Sale?

You need to find a creative solution that fits the seller's needs and make a fair deal, like the example above where we could help the seller move on quickly. For example, we can cash advance in some cases money upfront upon signing of contracts.

Why would a seller do this?

They must be motivated and have a reason to move or sell quickly, this will not work with someone who has all the time in the world so pass these sellers on to an estate agent.

What paperwork is needed?

We use a simple Heads of Terms which details what has been agreed and then pass this to the solicitors who then draft the assisted sales contract, also a power of attorney document is used and a letter of authority so you can deal with the lenders, which is vital. This should be done before any cash advance is paid to the seller, you may be thinking well what's to stop the seller just running away with the cash advance, we use a RX1 restriction or charge to protect our interest in the deal which would block any sale.

Dave's Top Tips

Monetise all your seller leads and don't just offer an assisted sale, we have multiple strategies we can use to help sellers with property such as lease options (LO) or a Below Market Value offer (BMV), for non-motivated sellers you can also monetise these leads by passing them to a local agent and collecting a referral fee.

Always use a solicitor to check the property title and debt secured against the property as some sellers may be looking to offload a bad deal to you, always make sure you are protected.

Become a social worker, let sellers talk and unload their troubles and just listen.

Always be ethical, you will come across some deals you could do but shouldn't, put the seller first over profit as this will pay off long-term.

Look at adding value to deals which others miss, can you extend the lease to make it more profitable? will a refurb increase the value? etc.

David's Assisted Sale Case Study

We had a seller contact us from some of our marketing who told us they were moving to another county to work an and he wanted to sell his property as he had no wish to become a landlord. He also went on to explain that the sales market locally was slow and he may have to wait 3-4 months for a sale, if he waited this long he would have an empty property costing him insurance, mortgage payments, council tax and it would also be at risk of getting vandalised. Furthermore the property type was popular with investors and he would likely have to drop the price as investors always want a good deal, he also said he wanted to clear a tax bill for £7,875 which was the main thing he wanted from this transaction.

We put the figures into the calculator (see below) and worked out a deal where we could make £12,280 profit and we could give him his tax bill money in advance and we would take care of the sale for him, he signed the paperwork and we advanced him the funds

(£7,875).Once he had moved out of the property, we then advertised the property on Rightmove using an on line agent, their costs were very low (£840) which is great leverage for us as we don't have to worry about viewings and so on, we could focus on doing more deals.

We had budgeted the running costs (we are responsible for these) for 6 months so we knew we could easily sell it in the time frame as we had done our research and the profit was very predictable as we had done our due diligence properly.

So, we did a consultation with him, found out his pain points and what he wanted from the sale and structured a creative deal that was really win/win for all involved,
Estate agents are very set in their ways and would not know how to do something like this and this is why we look for problems and provide creative solutions for sellers who need a customised solution to their problems.

Assisted sale - Template			
Current Valuation		£	70,000.00
PP to vendor	75%	£	52,500.00
Mortgage 1		£	-
Mortgage 2			
Mortgage 3			
Total secured loans		£	-
Max Cash Advance		£	52,500.00
Actual Cash Advance		£	7,875.00	15%
Mortgage Arrears paid		£	-
Retained Cash		£	44,625.00
Costs			
Mortgage Arrears paid		£	-
MTG Payments	6	£	-
Running costs	£ 160.00	£	880.00
Finders Fee		£	-
Refurb			
Legal eviction costs		£	-
Monthly rent	£	-	
Total costs		£	880.00
TOTAL Capital req Inc Advance		£	8,755.00

Assisted sale - Selling			
OMV resale		£	70,000
Strike Price		£	65,000
Buying costs		£	53,380
Selling costs			
EA		£	840
Legal		£	1,000
Vendor Profit Share		£	2,500	50%
Total Costs		£	4,340
Profit		£	12,280
Deal Return	140%		

Jordan's Story

Jordan and Tegan were backpackers, originally from Wales who had travelled widely before living in Australia when they came across my YouTube channel and started watching my educational videos.

https://tinyurl.com/youtubedavidfrance

Jordan contacted me before coming on as a mentee in 2019.

During our initial discussion he revealed that he had a very interesting career in Australia as a skydiving instructor, where he was making decent money and life was good. However, he realised this would not be a long-term career and was planning on returning to Wales to get married and settle down. He did not want to get a 'normal' job and as he had always loved property he was thinking about taking this up to create an alternative income stream.

Jordan had a passion for property but he thought like most people that you need lots of money to get started, however after seeing some of my YouTube videos he realised this was not the case and he was able to get going right away using very little funds.

Jordan appreciated my no-BS approach and chose me as his mentor, I explained that this business requires work, focus and effort but can be very lucrative if you put the work in. He had done his research on various property training programs, but he was attracted by our one-on-one mentoring and hand-holding approach and the fact that we had a ready market of buyers to sell his deals on in a partnership arrangement.

Jordan chose property flipping /trading as a good way to start off in property with very little risk, his role was to find profitable property deals and secure them using the correct paperwork (no mortgages needed), then trade on that property to investors who would pay him thousands of pounds.

Jordan is now working on more adventurous deals and makes tens of thousands of pounds per property transaction.

He divides his time between skydiving at weekends and doing his property deals during the week.

Jordan's Assisted Sale Case Study

Wales - Assisted Sale Deal

Valuation £145,000
Price agreed with seller £112,000
Cash advance to seller £20,000 (comes off price agreed)
Legal fees/other £2,414
Total cash needed £22,414
Sold price £138,000
NET profit after costs £23,586

All Jordan did with the above was find a seller who needed the £20,000 quickly and agreed to sell the property for them and do all the running around. Jordan outlaid a total of £22,414 for 4 months and then got this back with £23,586 on top, deals this profitable are unusual but are out there, our typical profits on these types of deals are around £10,000-£15,000.

The Seller Finance Strategy Explained

Fancy a place in the sun? No deposit, no mortgage, no interest payable, then you will love this unique strategy.

With this strategy we flip these deals to people who want a home in the sun and collect £5,000 per deal, which buyers are happy to pay.

So how does it work?

We find a seller of a property who does not need all the money from the sale right now and is happy to be paid monthly, we agree a purchase price and spread the balance over 120-180 months usually with zero deposit, zero interest, and with no need for a mortgage, simple right!

One of the main reasons I went down this path of trading property deals internationally is I have a massive passion for world travel along with property and this seemed to fit in well. I first came across this strategy on Ebay and loved the fact the owner gives you an effective loan on the property, they are acting as the bank. The Americans have been doing this for many years but in the UK we are always slow to catch on. This is why this strategy is called Seller Finance, in essence the seller is financing the deal.

So far, we have done multiple deals in the following countries (remotely, from my home).

UK
Las Vegas, USA
Orlando Florida
Niagara, New York
Bodrum, Turkey
Paphos, Cyprus
Marbella, Spain (and many other areas of Spain)
Sharm el Shaikh, Egypt
Nova Scotia, Canada

Arkansas, USA
Memphis, Tennessee
And many more..

There are 196 Countries worldwide so how many deals do you think are out there?
And how many £5,000 deals do you need to do each month to replace your income?

Where do we find these deals?

Classified sites and FSBO (for sale by owner) are some of the best websites we use to get these deals, it's easy to reach people worldwide with the internet and by using classifieds you can get to the owner directly.

Where do we find the buyers?

We use some of the same places we get the sellers, however we redesign the listing to show that the purchase structure reflects seller finance.

How does the legal process work?

It is very important you use solicitors based in the country where the property is located, as they must understand the law of the land. In some countries certain taxes become due with instalment contracts (seller finance agreements), so legal variations must be used to either defer or avoid the tax, also many other potential issues can arise if you do not use the correct legal process.

Dave's Top Tips

Offer the seller the amounts over number of months rather than in years, i.e. 120 months not 10 years, sellers react better to it in this way.

This works best with little to no deposit payable to the owner, however some owners insist on a deposit so make sure you keep the deposit 10% or below, the main reason is if the deposit is too high then this loses its attractiveness and a buyer could just go and get a mortgage.

Do your due diligence on the solicitors and make sure they are part of the correct governing bodies, for example in the UK solicitors should be a member of The Law Society.

Currencies: make sure you are clear on what currency is to be used for your fee and the seller payments

Always go direct to vendor (D2V) with this strategy as when going via estate agents we find they explain this wrongly to the sellers and this can cause deals to fall over.

Properties under 400,000 (£$) work best for this as the monthly payments are more affordable when spread out.

Avoid France and Bulgaria as we have found these markets very difficult to do deals in because of the legal system

Next, see some of these deals we have done worldwide…

David's Seller Finance Deal (Paphos Cyprus)

- 2 Bedroom apartment
- NO MORTGAGE NEEDED
- NO INTEREST PAYABLE
- ANYONE CAN BUY
- £80,000 spread over 150 months
- Only £533 per month
- Just pay our fees and legal fees
- Communal swimming pool
- Recent sales are £90,000+
- Unfurnished
- Great location

OUR FEE £5,000

(our profit for putting the deal together)

David's Seller Finance Deal (Las Vegas, USA)

- 1 Bedroom condo
- NO MORTGAGE NEEDED
- NO INTEREST PAYABLE
- ANYONE CAN BUY
- £22,435 spread over 120 months
- Only £186 per month
- Just pay our fees and legal fees
- Unfurnished
- Great location

OUR FEE £5,000

(our profit for putting the deal together)

David's Seller Finance Deal (Lanzarote, Canary Islands)

- 4 Bedroom detached
- NO MORTGAGE NEEDED
- NO INTEREST PAYABLE
- ANYONE CAN BUY
- £289,880 spread over 120 months
- Only £1,999 per month with £50,000 balloon payment
- Just pay our fees and legal fees
- Unfurnished
- Great letting potential

OUR FEE £5,000

(our profit for putting the deal together)

David's Seller Finance Deal (Boat in France)

- Fairline Targa 40
- Boat docked in France (can ship wherever)
- Deposit to owner £33,000
- Monthly payment to owner £2,000 over 48 months
- Docked in France/Email for full spec

OUR FEE £5,000

(our profit for putting the deal together)

The Rent to Own Strategy

What is Rent to Own? As the name suggests you rent a property to a tenant but also give them the opportunity to own the property at the end of a fixed term.

How can we make money from this strategy?

If you have a property you own or control (lease option) then you can offer a tenant the chance to buy your property in the future by agreeing a price today, you would make money from building a fair margin (profit) into each deal.

Example

John has a property he has owned in his portfolio for 5 years, every 12 months on average a tenant moves out and the property is empty for 2-3 months, when a property is empty it turns into a liability and you have to pay expenses like mortgage payments, council tax and insurance. Also, when using a letting agent you have to pay tenant-finder fees which can be one month's rent, so over a five year term these costs can run into thousands of pounds.

The house John owns is worth £100,000 and the property rents for £600 a month.

John decides he wants a tenant buyer for the property, after doing some marketing John has some people that want to view the property, he finds someone who wanted to take it and the best part is the tenant is responsible for the repairs and maintenance and as they are going to be in the property usually for 5 years then you have no void periods thus increasing the overall cashflow.

The numbers look like this..

£100,000 purchase price with 7% added every year (compounded) until they buy and a rent of £600 a month over an agreed term of five years.

See the working example next...

Today's Market Value	£100,000	Established by an independent surveyor.
Option Agreement Term in Years	5	This can be used by the tenant to alter their monthly option payments
House Price Increase Multiplier	7%	This is set using historic price data
End of Option Term Forecast House Value	140,255	What our historic price data forecasts going forward.
Tenant Fixed Contribution	£5000	This is negotiable, used to secure the discounted deal.
Tenant Optional Additional Deposit		This can be used by the tenant to alter their monthly option payments
End of 5 Year Option Purchase Price Agreed With Landlord.	132,255	This value is based on minimum 5-year option term
Adjusted Net Purchase Price at End of Option Period	£132,255	This value applies pro-rata uplift associated with the extended option term.
Market Rent	£600	What could be achieved in the current market

So you can see the margin we have created with this strategy, if the tenant buys the property in year 5 then the profit will be £40,255 plus the cashflow up to that point, the national average annual increase in property value over 20-30 years is about 7% across the UK so we have taken a conservative and fair amount to add as capital uplift.

Also, you may have noticed you get paid a fee upfront which comes off the purchase price, in this case £5,000 this is the commitment fee from the tenant buyer and is non-refundable

What are the benefits to a tenant buyer?

They have security and peace of mind that they will not have to move and can buy the property inside the five year term, most will not be able to buy before this, due to needing to save for a deposit to buy the property and some have other challenges like IVA's and poor credit that they need to repair over time.

If a tenant has poor credit then this can be a great solution for them as they can rent the property, put their own stamp on the place and treat it like their own until they are ready to buy. By offering this unique concept the tenants will love you for it and pay you like clockwork every month as the legal agreements state if they miss consecutive payments, they forfeit the deal.

Where can you find a tenant buyer?

We use Rightmove and some of the big portals to get maximum exposure, you can also use low cost methods like newspapers, local shops, chip shops, bandit boards, classified websites like Gumtree, also leaflet drops can work well too.

What legal paperwork is used?

Always use a solicitor to do the paperwork but like a lease option you need a Heads of Terms which reflects the deal structure and the names of all parties involved, then the solicitors will usually issue a AST (assured shorthold tenancy agreement) and an option agreement (this states the purchase price) and sometimes an RX1 restriction is also used to further protect the tenant buyer (an RX1 gets put on the property title at the land registry and means the seller can't sell the property without consent of the tenant buyer)

Dave's top tips

Do block viewings as this builds scarcity and makes people want it even more as they think they will lose out.

When I first started doing this, I sent letters to my current tenants and asked if they wanted to buy the property in the future and rent until they can buy, I had three tenants take me up on this and pay me thousands of pounds up front.

Don't put tenant buyers in all your properties as if all the tenants do buy then you will lose out on long-term wealth generation with property, I do this on a few properties that have either a high turnover of tenants or cause a lot of maintenance issues.

If you are disposing of your property portfolio you can stagger the sales of the properties in line with CGT (capital gains tax) liabilities thus saving tax, just make sure you are clear with the tenant buyer when they can and can't buy and work out the best deal possible.

You can do these over any period of time you like but I suggest based on my experience 3 or 5 years only, as if you do them over too long a period, the tenant buyers may never get round to buying, if it is too short you don't make as much money as the compounding takes time to kick in.

Only ever let a tenant buyer in if they have a job and some upfront money, tenants claiming benefits will never be able to use this income to get a mortgage and if they have no upfront money they have no skin in the game and can walk away.

David's Rent to Own Case Study

We had this property in St Helens (see image above), on a lease option for a few years, it was attracting a lot of repairs and the letting agent we used was based a long way from the property and struggled to get tenants in as they were not local, so we decided to put in a tenant buyer.

The tenant buyer came from the advert we had on Rightmove, (see image 2), her name was Emma and she had a good job in the NHS but she had an IVA which would take over a year to clear, so she said this was perfect for her.

Emma paid us an advance and also covered the legal fees on her side, we decided as the property needed some fixing up to take a low amount upfront of £1,995 instead of £5,000.

The Deal

Emma has the property for three years with the right to buy it at £89,000 with 7% interest annually and a 2 year extension (with a £3,000 extension clause), as you can see you can structure the deals as you like as long as it is fair.

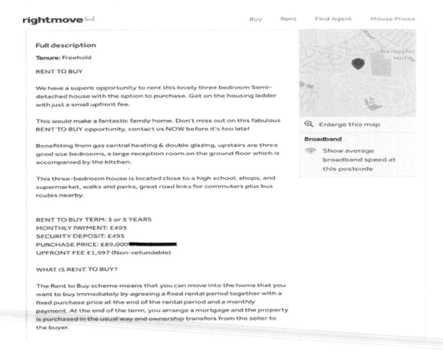

Portfolio Acquisitions Strategy

Why acquire a property portfolio?

It can take a long time to build a property portfolio even using some of the very creative property strategies so taking a whole property portfolio in one go can be a very good way of speeding up the whole process.

Portfolios range in size and location but usually the portfolio consists of good rental properties with the odd not-so-good one thrown in, this is what we have found when we have acquired property portfolios.

How can you make money with portfolios?

In exactly the same way as with one property! However you get great leverage as you can split the portfolio up and keep some, trade some or keep the whole lot.

Why do people sell property portfolios?

Right now (2020), many landlords are facing huge challenges as the government are trying to make it harder for landlords to make money by introducing something called section 24/ clause 24. This means people who hold property in their personal names as opposed to a company can no longer offset the interest part of the mortgage against rental income thus meaning they pay more tax.

Also, we find people selling portfolios for many other reasons, such as burnt out landlords, they take on too many properties and try to do everything themselves such as letting properties, which is a skilled job with lots of red tape, (that is why we never manage any of our properties we give them to letting agents as we know where the real money is and that is doing more property deals not dealing with blocked toilets).

Provide solutions and get what you want.

If a property portfolio owner wants to sell up he has only one type of buyer for the whole thing, an investor! If he sells them off one by one this can take months or years, also most investor buyers will want a discount. Furthermore if they sell a few properties then capital gains tax can eat most of the profits, so to buy using a creative purchase structure like a lease option means the seller can stagger any sales over a few years making use of capital gains tax relief which at the time of writing is currently £12,000 and if you have two owners you get £24,000 and so on.

This is just one of many ways to structure a deal to help a motivated portfolio seller, obviously you as an investor will want to make cashflow or a gain in some way from the portfolio, this is exactly what we teach our clients and support them with in our partner program.

How do you find property portfolios?

You can use many different channels but we find the landlord publications work well, also some newspapers like the FT can work as you will find most landlords with decent size portfolios are over 50 years old and read these sorts of publications. Think about what they do, read and how they act and try to reach them where they are.

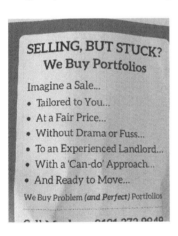

Dave's Top Tips

Only ever work with a motivated seller, like on any deal we do as otherwise you will waste a lot of time, portfolios are great but can take lots of time to work on doing the due diligence so it's only worth it if you know the seller is highly motivated.

Don't be afraid to pay the seller some equity now, you can advance equity under a lease option agreement as long as it's still a great deal.

Focus on ROCE not ROI, work out what cash you have to put in and how long it will take to get it back, we work on a rule that we must get all our cashback from any deal inside 12 months maximum, however on some deals we have got our initial funds back inside 3 months, this is one massive thing I learned where most people go wrong, trapping all your money in a property will mean your growth is restricted.

Portfolio Takeover Case Study

Phil.H was a burnt out landlord who came to us via some marketing. He had built a portfolio of around 17 houses, he was now 67 years old and fed up of bad tenants and repairs, he also worked full time as a truck driver and the problems were distracting him from his work and so he was highly motivated and ready to sell.

After getting all the details of his portfolio we structured a fair deal and realised he actually didn't need to sell as most properties had little to no equity and the ones that did have equity could get taken by the lenders, as some have a clause in their terms and conditions called an all monies charge where they can claim some of the benefit from one property to offset against losses on the others.

Knowing this, we were able to work out a deal where we could advance some equity to Phil under a lease option structure, meaning he gets some money now and then we sold the whole portfolio to an international client. We introduced the client to some letting agents to manage the portfolio and they get cash flow every month from these (circa £4,500) and we got a big broker fee for putting this deal together, so everyone in the deal was a winner. The best part is no mortgages were needed in this case and the investors only had pay out £70,000 plus legal fees, if they bought how most people usually buy using deposits they would have needed £510,000 to put down in deposits!!

You see most sellers think they need to sell, but most don't, like Phil what they need is our expertise combined with creative strategies to create win-win scenarios for all parties.

How to Choose the RIGHT Property Path for You

You have been lied to! You do not need lots of money to be successful in property as you will have seen from my story and those of my students using some of the strategies we have discussed in this book, I have cut out any fluff you get in a lot of property books to get straight to the point.

You have no excuses not to take action, you owe it to yourself and your loved ones!

Let's face it, all the strategies we cover in this book can make you money but how do you know which one is right for you?

Maybe you hate your job and want to replace your income, maybe you love your job but want to leave a legacy for your family.

It can be very overwhelming starting out in property and very easy to go down the wrong path for you, I lost lots of time by chasing 'shiny pennies' I knew I could get a mentor who has been there and done what I wanted to do, but thinking I could do it myself cost me years of my life.

You pay the price one way or another, either pay to learn and follow a proven system or try and do it yourself which could mean you lose everything or it could take you decades before you make it!

Let me ask you a question, does it make more sense for you to go through what I had to, all the years of trial and error by 'going it alone 'and possibly many thousands wasted in making mistakes, (this can be extremely costly), or is it more sensible to have a mentor who's been where you are now and who can give you the advice and handholding to get to your end goal in 1-2 years whilst also being able to leverage their experience, contacts and funding?

Why not book a free 30 minute strategy session with me using the link below and let's get crystal clear on what you want and what you don't want and see if we can help you.

You can email me at: **dave@portfoliomillionaire.com**

https://tinyurl.com/strategy-call

Free Training Course

https://tinyurl.com/4daysfreetraining

Free Deal Calculator

https://tinyurl.com/leaseoptiontoolkit

Educational YouTube Channel

YouTube
https://tinyurl.com/youtubedavidfrance

You can also contact me in the following ways

LinkedIn
https://tinyurl.com/linked-in

Facebook
https://tinyurl.com/davidfrancefacebook

Printed in Great Britain
by Amazon

57389863R00038